—Balsamic viniger

W9-AQB-958

Table of Contents

❖

mexican chicken soup – 43

— Buffalo chicken soup pg 41
3 tbs ranch
1 cup Buffalo hot sense
4 cup cheddar cheese
* shredded*
5 cupps chicken broth
onion
soups pg 42 ? pork stock

Nowadays there are numerous modern methods of cooking, which were creatively devised to diminish cooking time while conserving nutritious quality and among these is the Instant Pot. An Instant Pot is a programmable electric pressure cooker that is capable of doing the work of various kitchen gadgets; this appliance allows you to program cooking up to 24 hours in advanced and has other convenient functions that are pre-programmed for easy use! The pressure from an Instant pot is created after you boil a liquid, as an example water or broth, inside the sealed pressure cooker. This then creates and traps steam, which generates an internal pressure and heat, which then cooks the food within a short time. Genius, isn't it? After cooking, you should slowly release the pressure before you open the vessel to prevent injuries from hot steam; this is especially important to note for people who have never used an Instant Pot before.

As opposed to the majority of other pressure cookers, an Instant Pot usually has an entire stainless-steel interior that is in contact with your food. This ensures that non-stick material don't get cooked and contaminate your food. In short there's no non-stick or Teflon surface so there won't be any toxic fumes coming out when the insides heat up high. As the cooking bowl is made from stainless steel materials, it's easy for you to clean by hand or through using a dishwasher. Now for a quick overview of the functions, an Instant Pot is a 7 in 1 programmable electric pressure cooker; it can work as a basic pressure cooker, sauté pan, slow cooker, yoghurt-maker, rice cooker, steamer and warmer. Before we get a bit further here, let us delve into the history and understand better how they were developed so we might not only enjoy their benefits, but appreciate their developmental history as well.

Instant Pot Cookbook

The Quick And Easy Pressure Cooker Guide For Smart People – Healthy, Easy, And Delicious Instant Pot Recipes

Madison Rose

Introduction

Dear Reader,

Ever since I was a youthful kid, I have been downright passionate with creating mouthwatering food recipes. I would spend countless hours each day trying to muster up picture-perfect recipes to amaze not only my family and friends but the world as well. Needless to say, along the road I did have my fair share of bumps and bruises but in the end, I was able to get a superb grasp on culinary arts.

To begin, I'd like to applaud and congratulate you for grabbing this book, *"Instant Pot Cookbook: The Quick And Easy Pressure Cooker Guide For Smart People – Healthy, Easy, And Delicious Instant Pot Recipes."* This book has comprehensive information about the Instant Pot along with loads of my hand crafted, healthy, easy, and delicious Instant Pot recipes to get you started on your way to amazing meals and more.

In the busy world we live in today, everything is about convenience. We've all got so much on our plates that we hardly have time to attend the more important things in life, never mind cooking. Unfortunately, that's where most of us end up opting for convenience and making poor lifestyle choices which ends up costing us our health, which in turn, detriments the quality of not only our lives, but the lives of the people around us as well. Think about it; when cooking seems more like a chore that takes up a decent chunk of your time, you just might not fathom having to prepare foods for more than an hour after spending long hard hours at work. What's much more convenient for many of us is to go to fast food joints to buy French fries and burgers or anything of that sort. However, as we all well know, many of these foods are unhealthy, yet we continue eating them just because they are simply easy and time savers.

So what's the solution to that? Well, simple, if you want to bring fun to cooking while ensuring that you eat healthy and have lots of time left over to spare, you have to try the Instant Pot. Created with busy people in mind, this cookware is undoubtedly the one thing you need to stop relying heavily on fast food and in addition, to ensure that you don't end up spending too much time preparing your meals. If you are looking for comprehensive information about the Instant Pot such as what it is, how it works, how it can make your life easy, how it came into being, along with tons of delicious recipes that you can prepare today, this book has it all. After reading this book, you should be able to use the Instant Pot like a true professional to streamline your life and add flavor to your meals.

Thanks again for joining in on this life-changing journey. I hope you success in creating more time, health, and fun in your life.

Sincerely,
Madison Rose

History Of The Instant Pot

❖

Before the Instant Pot took its first steps on Earth, there were basic pressure-cooking devices being experimented and tested; the first pressure cooker was actually developed in 1679 by a French physicist Denis Papin in a bid to save fuel and time while cooking foods, in particular, meat. When Denis presented his invention, members of the Royal Society of London treated the discovery as an ordinary scientific study though he was granted membership to the society. Little did the members know what a movement this invention would fashion down the road of time.

Next, Georg Gutbrod from Stuttgart in 1864 started to make his own pressure cookers from tinned cast iron. These were followed by a Zaragoza version made by Jose Alix Martínez, which was labeled as "express cooking pot". In 1924, a recipe book for cooking with pressure cookers was written by José Alix and was published. Later in 1938, Alfred Vischer from New York created a gadget called the Flex-Seal Speed Cooker, which was designed, for regular use in regular homes. A short year later, a company known as the "National Pressure Cooker Company", designed their own commercial version of pressure cookers, which were still stovetops.

The electric version of pressure cookers wasn't invented until a few decades back by a Chinese scientist called Yong-Guang Wang, in 1991. These types of pressure cookers are also known as 3rd generation pressure cookers.

Following the electric pressure cookers came the Instant Pot, which is a programmable multi-cooker that can do the combined tasks of many appliances based on the different settings of pressure, temperature and the duration of cooking.

Parts And Design

I understand we're all impatiently excited about skipping to all the different functions of the Instant Pot and the tasty instructions but just before that, it's important we get a clear understanding into all the specifics of the cooker. Here is a detailed illustration of the many parts in an Instant Pot:

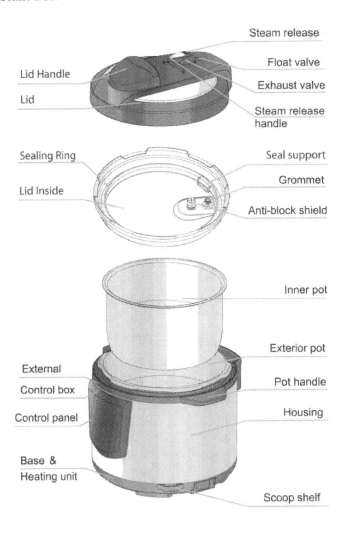

The basic parts of this device are the inner pot and the lid that comes with a locking device feature, which hinders the cooker from opening while under high pressure. The sealing ring also known as the gasket helps to seal the cooker airtight, while the steam vent has a pressure regulator on top that maintains the pressure in the inner pot. The cooker also features safety devices on the lid to control excess pressure or temperatures and a pressure indicator pin to detect the presence or absence of pressure. Common accessories to use along side this pressure cooker include a steamer basket, a trivet that keeps the steamer basket on top of any liquids and also a metal divider that separates foods.

INNER POT

Most pressure cookers, in particular 1st and 2nd generation pressure cookers, have inner pots which are made from either aluminum or stainless steel. If the pressure cooker is made from aluminum, exercise caution as it could be reactive to acidic foods, and can alter the flavor in foods. Those made from stainless steel such as the Instant Pot comprise of a heavy 3 layer or heat spreader that facilitate uniform heating since steel has a lower thermal conductivity. As opposed to aluminum made cookers, stainless steel is dishwasher safe.

SEALING RING / GASKET

The sealing ring is made from a silicon compound, and helps create a gas-tight seal that prevents steam or air to escape from the pan and the lid. Basically, the only place steam can escape is through the regulator found on the lid. In case the regulator is blocked, a safety valve is designed to offer backup escape for the steam. The design of this pressure cooker makes it both safe and effective for the common household.

STEAM OR PRESSURE RELEASE VALVE

This functionality detects when the cooker is about to build pressure and also when the pressure is excess or should be released. The steam release valve may depend on how fast you release the pressure in case a recipe calls for it, which is very convenient! When the cooker comes to build a lot of pressure, sometimes you'll notice steam escaping through this valve, which is absolutely fine, in the majority of cases, it's just a safety precaution. The value can also serves as a pressure indicator, thus it should always remain clean.

FILL LINES

This is a labeling inside the cooking pot where it depicts the minimum and maximum fill lines.

Now that you know the gist of the history and how the Instant Pot came into being and the different parts, let us look at how you can benefit with having one of these amazing appliances.

Benefits Of Instant Pot

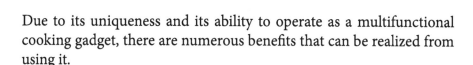

Due to its uniqueness and its ability to operate as a multifunctional cooking gadget, there are numerous benefits that can be realized from using it.

It is faster

Owing to the Instant Pot's ability in creating a sealed environment where there is adequate pressure to cook, it takes a shorter time to complete a similar job using a different method. For instance, using the stove, you can cook beans for over two hours. However, with an Instant Pot, you may only need 45 minutes or even less to do the same job. What does this equate to? You can have the same meal done and have time to spare for your other important tasks. Enjoy your extra free time!

It saves energy

An Instant Pot is built in a way that it doesn't require a separate gas or an electric stove, to cook for long periods of time, in a bid to save energy. Instead, it has an insulated external pot and uses very little water in cooking, making it a better energy saver than even the microwave. Statistics show that this method helps you save more energy by up to 70 percent as compared to other cooking gadgets. Its ability to save energy is also linked to it being very fast. Cool isn't it?

Preserves nutrients and cooks tasty food

Research shows that when cooking with pressure, heat is supplied evenly, deeply and is easily distributed. In addition, you don't even have to immerse food in lots of water; just a little amount to help the cooker supply enough steam to the food is enough. As food is steamed, most vitamins and minerals aren't destroyed or dissolved away by the cooking water as in other cookers and other cooking methods. The steam also surrounds the food and thus ingredients aren't easily oxidized through exposure to air. Foods such as broccoli and asparagus do not require a lot of heat to cook and thus an Instant Pot can help them retain their nutrients and more of their green coloring.

Furthermore, Instant Pot's are fully sealed to ensure that no steam or smell can spread throughout your home or kitchen. The concept is designed to make sure that your home remains smelling the same and the food remains tasty with their original flavor.

Kills harmful microorganisms in food

When in use, your food is cooked at a temperature setting higher than the boiling point of water, which eventually denatures microorganisms like viruses and bacteria. Thus, an Instant Pot can at the same time serve as a sterilizer say for glass baby bottles or jam pots.

In some cases, foods such as beans, corn, wheat and rice carry fungal poisons referred to as aflatoxins. These are mycotoxins that occur naturally from the reproduction of Aspergillus fungi, mainly as a result of poor storage and humid conditions. These toxins can cause various complications among them liver cancer and can trigger other cancers as well. Usually, heating food to the boiling point of water doesn't necessarily kill all aflatoxins, however, an Instant Pot helps reduce its amount to a safe level. Kidney beans on the other hand have a toxin referred to as phytohaemagglutinin, but can easily be destroyed when water is heated at high temperatures for 10 minutes, and you can set that automatically with this multifunctional cooker.

It is safe to use

One of the most common fears associated with pressure cookers and the Instant Pot is the likelihood in burning yourself while cooking as it may release steam leading to severe burns. However, when used correctly, these cookers are actually safe and well sealed to prevent possible accidents; all you need to do is keep them away from objects that can tamper with its lid. Furthermore, Instant Pot's are extremely easy to use and only require a little time to get accustomed to it. All you need to do is read the manual and then get your meals ready!

Has a lower PSI

Stovetop pressure cookers normally work at 15 PSI, whereas electric cookers such as the Instant Pot have a lower range of 10-12 PSI. The lower pressure point setting helps them cook more efficiently but also causes them to cook slightly slower than their stovetop counterparts. To bring an Instant Pot to 12psi, it would take you around 5 minutes to heat a cup of cold water in order to bring it to pressure. In case you need to cook a large pot that is full of liquid say stew, you might need around 15 minutes to bring the pot to pressure. That said; electric pressure cookers and the Instant Pot are easier to handle and don't require constant monitoring.

Cheaper

Considering that this appliance can do a number of different functions, by simply purchasing one, you don't need to buy several other gadgets, such as the rice cooker. Therefore, this greatly saves you not only on room space but also on costs. Amazing isn't it?

What To Watch Out For Before Buying An Instant Pot

Despite Instant Pot pressure cookers being astonishing appliances, they also have their own pitfalls that you need to be aware of if you want to have a great time using them. These include:

- Most models are a bit more expensive than the average electric pressure cookers during the initial purchase and in replacing the parts, especially the lids. Generally they are quite durable but if your environment requires you to shuffle things around constantly, just be careful in avoid damaging it.

- Instant pots can be relatively large and may not fit well in small cabinets. A simple trick is to store it on top of the fridge.

- The inner pot may be non-stick, depending on which model you get, which can easily get damaged and compromises your food flavor or smells. Thus, it's a wise idea to be replacing the cooking pot pretty soon if your Instant Pot is used fairly often, or to just choose the other models with the stainless steel; there are pros and cons with both ways.

- It takes some time to come to pressure and this might delay your cooking time. A few foods may demand longer cooking times for this reason.

- You have limited control over temperature, as you're only provided with programmed pressure cooker settings!

- Depending on which model you purchase, the Instant Pot can have new or older features. For example, if you want to use the Sauté function, you will need the new IP-LUX or IP-DUO series.

The Art Of Cooking: How To Use The Instant Pot

7 Easy Steps To Pressure Cooking with the Instant Pot

Hopefully now you have an Instant Pot and are ready to learn how to operate it. It is exciting to unwrap one and to see all the different features and gadgets; it is even more exciting to learn how simple this machinery will make your life simpler.

This pressure cooker is very simple to use and we will go over the basics here.

1) **Decide the length of time required to cook your meal**
   This is very straightforward and doesn't have any hidden meanings. Simply determine the time needed to cook the meal you have chosen. Remember, the differences between under cooking and over cooking can have an enormous effect on the flavor, texture, and appearance of your dish; in order to master the art of cooking with the Instant Pot; you must get the time correct.

   There are two great recommendations we can make here with regards to this area.

   a) Recipe Book – you have already purchased this recipe book so there are lots of delicious healthy recipes included with the required time included. Enjoy!
   b) There is a great appendix on the Instant Pot website that lists the cooking times for most commonly cooked foods. You can reach the website at www.InstantPot.com and click on "Cooking Times."

2) **Lid is clean and ready**

Make sure that the lid is clean and ready for use. There are 3 components to this part.

a) Sealing ring is clean and properly installed
b) Float Valve is clean and easily goes up and down
c) Steam release handle is clean and pointing to the ceiling position.

When you first use the Instant Pot, check each of these to ensure the lid is ready and subsequently, check them before any meals.

3) **Place food in inner pot**

This step can seem to be very easy but there are just a few things to watch out for. You must be thinking, "What else could there be to it?" It's quite simple, but just watch out for these.

a) If the size of your meal can help it, try and position it into the center without it touching the edges.
b) Depending if the size of your meal requires it, use a trivet.

These are just to ensure that your meal is cooked evenly and are just a few extra steps in making that perfect meal.

4) **Install Lid** – turn clockwise to the lock position

This part is pretty self-explanatory. When everything is in position, simply turn clockwise until the lid is in lock position.

5) **Plug the unit it** – should hear a beep when you plug it in

    That's right, you're nearing the completion of the steps and step 5 is as simple as plugging the unit it! Just make sure you hear the beeping sound that will occur as you plug your unit in.

6) **Select one of the different functions**

Now, down to the main reason why this multifunctional pressure cooker is loved by so many, it's an all-in-one machine! There are so many different combinations you can use that this is literally all you need to cook pretty much all your meals!

There are multiple different functions of using this pressure cooker and we'll go over them each one by one for you to learn exactly how best to use them. Many people get excited when they find out what all they can do is, so let's get down right to it and learn all these exciting features.

First off comes the control panel shown below.

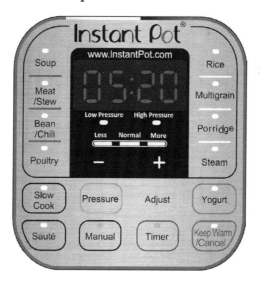

The control panel on an Instant Pot

FUNCTIONS

Soup

This function is pre-set to high pressure and has a default time of 30 minutes. Depending on your desired cook time, you can press the "adjust" button to tweak the time you desire for 40 minutes or 20 minutes.

Poultry

This function is pre-set to high pressure and has a default time of 15 minutes. Depending on your desired cook time, you can press the "adjust" button to tweak the time you desire for 30 minutes or 5 minutes.

Meat/Stew

This function is pre-set to high pressure and has a default time of 35 minutes. Depending on your desired cook time, you can press the "adjust" button to tweak the time you desire for 45 minutes or 20 minutes.

Bean/Chili

This function is pre-set to high pressure and has a default time of 30 minutes. Depending on your desired cook time, you can press the "adjust" button to tweak the time you desire for 40 minutes or 25 minutes.

Sauté

This function is to be used with the lid completely off and has a pre-set time of 30 minutes, which cannot be changed. Through using the "adjust" button, you can tweak your preference for more browning or less for a simmer.

Rice

The Rice function key is the only fully automatic function of the Instant Pot and requires no adjustments whatsoever. When you first press the rice function, you'll see the number 10, but that's not the time it'll take to cook. The pressure-cooking time for the rice feature will only show up after the pre-heat cycle. The time will be adjusted with how much you put into the pot, amazing it? You simply push the rice function, and then walk away.

Multi-grain

This function is pre-set to high pressure and has a default time of 40 minutes. Depending on your desired cook time, you can press the "adjust" button to tweak the time you desire for 60 minutes or 20 minutes.

Congee/Porridge

This function is pre-set to high pressure and has a default time of 20 minutes. Depending on your desired cook time, you can press the "adjust" button to tweak the time you desire for 30 minutes or 15 minutes.

Make a note, don't perform the quick release for congee/porridge or any other sticky foods, otherwise it will cause the food to squirt out of the steam release valves.

Steam

This function is pre-set to high pressure and has a default time of 10 minutes. Depending on your desired cook time, you can press the "adjust" button to tweak the time you desire for 15 minutes or 3 minutes.

One note to make when using the Steam function is to use a wire rack/ rack basket. During the steaming process, your meal will be cooked at full power uninterruptedly and during this period of time, you don't want your meal to be in direct contact with the pot.

Slow Cook

This function has a default time of 4 hours. Depending on your desired cook time, you can press the "+" and "-" button to tweak to your desired time.

Yogurt

This is a unique function and another reason why people choose the Instant Pot over other electric cooker brands.

To make Yogurt, there are generally a few different steps; we'll go over the essential ones here.

1. Sanitize the pot - This is very easy and you need to do is steam one cup of water for about a minute.
2. Boil the milk – through using the "adjust" button, wait until you see the screen showing "boil." Next, wait until this process is finished, which then the screen will show "Yogt."
3. Wait until the temperature drops a bit, which should take approximately 25 minutes.
4. Add your store bought yogurt to the milk
5. Press the "Yogurt" function again – this time, leave it and let it run for the default time of 8 hours.

Manual function – choose the time desired – maximum time is 120 minutes. This is to be used if you want a very specific time that isn't in part of the "pre-set" functions.

Timer – This is the delayed cooking function and can be used to delay cooking up to 24 hours. As a quick example, if you start the delayed time at 9am and set for 8 hours, your meal will be done by 5pm.

Keep Warm – In general, you should leave the "Keep Warm" function on, unless for a specific recipe, you require it to be turned off. The "Keep Warm" function will keep your food warm even after the cooking time is finished for up to 10 hours; this way, you won't have to rush back, and your meal will be warm even if you are late by an hour or two. Neat isn't it?

7) **Depressurize before opening**

Once done with the cooking time, it's time to release the pressure either quickly or naturally. For natural release, just turn off the pressure cooker and then wait for around 10-20 minutes for the pressure value on the indicator to drop. To release pressure quickly, just push the steam release valve handle to either the left or right. Don't use bare hands as the steam can be released instantly and cause serious burns. It is important to instruct children and people who are unfamiliar with how to use a pressure cooker of this aspect. Once the pressure on the indicator has dropped, you can open the pot safely.

a) *Natural Release Method* – Let the cooker sit for 10 to 20 minutes depending on how much food there is– even if it's on the keep warm cycle. You can place a cold wet towel on top to cool it down to speed this process up.

b) *Quick Release Method* – For a quicker method, turn the steam release handle to the right or left. Make sure that during this process, you're using a cooking mitt or towel and be very careful; steam that comes out will be very hot and can cause serious burns if not careful.

Here are some general things to keep in mind when using the Instant Pot

1. The time settings must be pressed within 10 seconds of pressing the function key, after the 10-second mark, it is set.

2. When you hear the first beep, the food will enter into the pre-heat cycle.

3. Once it reaches the optimum pressure, you'll see steam coming out, for 30 seconds to 2 minutes so don't be alarmed.

4. There are 10 proven safety mechanism to prevent the Instant Pot from having the accidents that first generation pressure cookers had, so don't be worried, it's very safe.

5) Once the cook time is up, your Instant Pot will beep, then go into the "keep warm" mode, incase you are doing something else at the time, for up to 10 hours.

An Instant Pot can be used for a variety of tasks depending on what you are cooking up! Let's see how you can prepare different foods and make them tasty and delicious with a few quick examples.

- Rice

As you know now, an Instant Pot can function as a high-capacity rice cooker since it has an automated rice-cooking program that should prepare your white rice within 10 minutes! Amazing isn't it? Brown rice takes longer to cook, around 25 minutes, which is not so bad when you compare it with traditional methods.

- Whole chicken

Due to the large capacity available, you can easily fit a whole medium-sized chicken. Within 45 minutes, the chicken should be tender and ready. It is advisable to position it on a wire stand rack insert to ensure it doesn't touch the bottom of the pot.

- Fish/Bone/Veggie stock

Basically you'll need around 2 hours using an Instant Pot to get a rich bone stock. If you are dealing with larger bones, 4 hours is recommended to allow two cycles of boiling. If this is too long for you, you can prepare the stock while you sleep!

- Lentils/beans/spit peas

The good part is that beans require the shortest cooking time of 10-15 minutes and often yields a smooth and tender texture. Lentils on the other hand can break down within 15 minutes or so to produce lentil soup or stew. Spit peas are best prepared on an Instant Pot as they easily soften up after a prolonged period of cooking.

- Stews

One good thing about this appliance is that it allows you to brown meat or veggies before you add in the liquids. Doing so helps simplify both the cooking and the cleaning process, and in addition, it also produces a richer flavored stew.

- Pot roast

Don't forget the slow cooker function, which best suites pot roasts. Use the Instant Pot in this case as you would use any slow cooker or crockpot.

- Beets and artichokes

Already frustrated that beets and artichokes take forever to steam or boil? An Instant Pot cooker should take you around 18-20 minutes to fix these ready.

Differences In Pressure Cookers

The stovetop pressure cooker was the predecessor to the modern electric Instant pot and actually takes a shorter time in the natural pressure release process than its counterpart. This is due to the Instant Pot's thermos-like double-walled construction that insulates against heat loss; hence, the modern cooker needs a longer time to allow the electric coil to cool down. The thermos-like double-walled build of the pressure cooker helps boosts efficiency as the insulation helps preserve heat, and this is why these pressure cookers in specific, are about 60 percent more energy efficient than stove top pressure cookers.

The stovetop version of a pressure cooker compared to an electric Instant Pot pressure cooker

Another notable difference between the two is the maximum amount of pressure that you can achieve. While stovetops operate up to 21 PSI depending on if you get a high-end model, an Instant Pot's pressure is around 11 PSI depending on which model you get. In a nutshell, lower pressure (lower PSI) in a cooker only means that you'll require more time to cook and thus you should as well adjust the cooking time in recipes that use different pressure cookers than the Instant Pot. That said, both versions could still save power, time and the nutritional value of food when comparing with traditional cooking methods, thus be free to choose any of the versions based on your preference. These are some other considerations that may influence your decision:

The pressure settings

Instant Pot's normally have two pressure settings, i.e. the High Pressure setting with ~10.2-11.6 PSI and a Low Pressure that ranges between ~5.8-7.2 PSI. To set the pressure, you simply need press the "Pressure" button and it'll alternate between High and Low. If you use any of the pre-set functions such as "Poultry", it'll auto-set for high pressure, except for the "Rice" function which is pre-set set for low.

Heat regulation

In a stovetop pressure cooker, you need to manually adjust the heat until the cooker reaches pressure. That said; sometimes you may need to try out different heat settings that prevent the cooker from losing or over-clocking pressure. An Instant Pot on the other hand is automated and thus, all you really need to do is choose the required pressure or a program like "meat" settings and then press "start", it's that simple. A stovetop pressure may require about 11 minutes to pressure up while an electric pressure cooker needs about 14 minutes like the Instant Pot. Time to pressure in an Instant Pot however depends on the wattage of electric heat coil (model based) as well as the fill level (amount of food you put into the pot).

Opening methods

A stovetop pressure cooker requires about 30 seconds for a cold — water quick release and 10 minutes for natural release. The Instant Pot pressure cooker recommends that you wait a minimum of 15-20 minutes for a natural release though this largely depends on the make or model of the cooker. However, for foods that foam during cooking, such as fruits, grains or legumes shouldn't be released via the quick release method, only use natural releases for these foods or else the food may quirt out of the valves.

Most other electric cookers on the other hand requires that you wait 3 minutes for a quick release, and approximately 25 minutes for natural releases.

Timer and cooking programs

A majority of stovetop pressure cookers don't have an interpreted timer and thus demands that you have a separate timer in order to track its cooking time. Furthermore, most don't have scheduling features or cooking programs, though you can use them together with an induction burner. Here the timer from the burner can help semi-automate a stovetop cooker by triggering natural release or turning it off.

Electric pressure cookers such as the Instant Pot on the other hand have an integrated timer to help track cooking time while cooking under pressure. When your cooker reaches the time limit, the timer will automatically countdown cooking time and switch off accordingly. This cooker also features a microcomputer controlled program that interacts with a thermostat and pressure sensor. For instance, the "Rice" function is completely automatic and the internal sensors decide how much time is required to prepare the rice. These cookers can allow you to schedule and delay cooking by up to 24 hours, so you can pretty much have your dinner done on the night before!

Safety

Most stovetop pressure cookers use a lid-locking system while cooking under pressure in order to inhibit you from opening the cooker. Also a primary over-pressure release valve can release excess pressure in case things get out of hand. Another secondary over-pressure release valve also helps you activate the pressure release in case the primary functionality fails. Furthermore, there's an emergency gasket pressure release that releases pressure down the body of the cooker or through a cutout lip of the lid.

An Instant Pot has a lid closure detection through a sensor, with a similar lid-locking system which works even when you've un-plugged the cooker. It also features a primary and secondary over-pressure release valve and an emergency gasket pressure release to help release pressure if it overbuilds. There is also a leaky lid detection done via the sensor that detects how long the cooker requires to reach the desired pressure, and hence switch to the "Keep Warm" feature to when applicable. In most cases the power protection or extreme temperatures can disconnect the cooker where there's overheating. Such automated control of temperature is monitored through an automated computer, in a bid to stop buildup of excess pressure.

Multi-uses

You can use the base of a stovetop pressure cooker as a cooking pot without the use of the pressure-cooking lid. For the larger models, you can use it for pressure canning of low-acid foods such as soups, vegetables and meat. The Instant Pot on the other hand cannot do pressure canning but it does includes a slow cooker and other multi-use programs as you learned earlier, which vastly outweighs the options available in traditional stovetops.

Storage

A regular stovetop pressure cooker can be stored with cooking pots and pans; an Instant Pot requires its own counter space and can be a bit tall and bulky, thus it's normally harder to store in a cupboard. Also ensure when under use that the cooker is not under an over-head cupboard as the steam can cause molding if it is directly beneath it.

Heat source

A stovetop cooker can be used on halogen, electric, gas, ceramic, induction, BBQ, camping stove or glass cook-tops. For the Instant Pot, the integrated electric coil is automatically turned on or off in response to an electrical circuit.

Materials and durability

Most stovetop pressure cookers are made of stainless steel, meaning that they are durable and usually take as long as 20 years to get damaged. Instant Pot's are also designed to be extremely durable as they're made of the same stainless steel. In these cases, all you may need to replace are the silicon parts like the gaskets. You'll require to replace the non-stick pots after frequent uses if you choose these additional parts; the other materials are quite durable and don't require much maintenance asides from making sure they're clean.

How To Clean Your Instant Pot

It's advisable to wash the cooker once done with cooking in order to prevent foods from drying or blocking parts of the device. Parts like valves, pressure indicators or steam vents need to be cleaned and rinsed regularly to ensure that foods are cooked accordingly and properly. Also remember to rinse the underside of the lid once done with cooking to prevent clogging of food materials. Do not soak the Instant Pot in sink water or in a dishwasher to avoid possible corrosion and electric circuit malfunctions.

For the lid and gasket, only wash them by hand and with cold water to avoid deforming the gasket. Be gentle with the gasket in order not to tear it or pull it off. In the event that the gasket has little cracks, is very sticky to handle or feels harder than usual, replace it with a new one! No doubt it's starting to become defective.

If you want to sanitize the inner pot, you can do so just by steaming water inside for about a minute.

Delicious, Easy And Healthy
Instant Pot Recipes

There is an old adage, "You are what you eat." There is a lot of wisdom packed into that line and it's true; the less nutritious food you eat (fast food), the more your body deteriorates and succumbs to illness easier and vice versa. The problem though that we face is that healthy food just doesn't taste good. Or does it?

I've packed here great delicious recipes that are not only favored by your taste buds, but your health as well! I implore you to try some, if not all, of the recipes here and create not only a healthier life style, but also more time to enjoy life as you simplify processes with the Instant Pot.

Good luck and enjoy!

Breakfast Recipes

———— ❖ ————

Creamy Coconut Oats

Serves 4

Ingredients

    1 cup steel cut oats

    ½ cup unsweetened coconut flakes

    1 pinch of salt

    2 cups water

    1 ¼ cup coconut milk plus more for topping

    1 cinnamon stick

    3 tablespoons brown sugar

Directions

1. Toast the coconut flakes by adding it into the Instant Pot, then select the "Sauté" button and cook for 6 minutes, ensuring to stir frequently. Watch closely to prevent burning.

2. Once the coconut flakes start to become a little brown, remove half of them and set them aside for the topping, then add the 1 cup steal cut oats into the Instant Pot to toast as well.

3. Cook the coconut flakes and oats for 3-5 minutes again using "Sauté" until they become scented then add 1 cup of coconut milk, reserving the remaining for the topping.

4. Add the rest of the ingredients (1 pinch salt, 1 cinnamon stick, 3 tablespoons brown sugar), while simultaneously stirring to mix. Press "Cancel" to stop "Sauté" then close the lid and press "manual" to choose 2 minutes and also select the "High Pressure" setting.

5. Once the 2 minutes are over, allow around 10 minutes for a natural pressure release then open the valve and lid. Serve this warm, topped with the remaining toasted coconut flakes and drizzle (¼ cup) coconut milk then enjoy.

Breakfast Quinoa

Serves 6

Ingredients

   1 pinch of salt

   ¼ teaspoon ground cinnamon

   ¾ teaspoon vanilla

   2 ½ tablespoons maple syrup

   2 ½ cups water

   1 ½ cups quinoa, uncooked and well rinsed

   ½ diced almonds

   ½ blueberries

   ¼ cup milk

Directions

1. Into the Instant Pot, add in ¼ teaspoon ground cinnamon, ¾ teaspoon vanilla, 2 ½ tablespoons maple syrup, 2 ½ cups water, 1 ½ cups quinoa, and 1 pinch of salt.

2. Select high-pressure on the control panel and cook for 1 full minute then when it finishes, let it natural release the pressure for around ten minutes then use the quick release to discharge any lingering pressure.

3. After opening the lid, tilt the lid away from you to let the steam escape.

4. Now fluff the quinoa and then serve it hot with diced almonds, blueberries and milk.

Enjoy!

Egg Muffins

Serves 2

Ingredients

6 slices precooked bacon, diced

1 green onion, slice and diced

4 tablespoons cheddar cheese, shredded

¼ teaspoon lemon pepper seasoning

4 eggs

Directions

1. Add 1 ½ cups of water then a steamer basket as well, into the Instant Pot.

2. Into a large measuring bowl that has a pour spout, break the 4 eggs and then add in ¼ teaspoon lemon pepper. Stir well.

3. Now divide the green onion, bacon and cheese over 4 silicon muffin cups. Then pour the beaten eggs evenly into every cup and use a fork to stir the mixture.

4. Into the steamer basket, put the muffin cups and then cover and lock the lid.

5. Select high pressure and 9 minutes cook time. When the beep sounds, wait for 3 minutes then quick release the pressure.

6. Open the lid carefully; remove the steamer basket alongside the muffin cups.

7. You can either serve instantly or keep the muffin cups in the fridge for up to 7 days. To serve the cups when chilled, microwave for around 20-40 seconds to reheat.

Hard-Boiled Eggs

Serves 4

Ingredients

> 4 cups cold water
>
> 8 fresh eggs
>
> 2 cups water or more

Directions

1. Fill your pressure cooker with 4 cups of cold water and insert the eggs into the steamer basket and place it above the water.

2. Completely secure the lid.

3. Steam the eggs for 6 minutes before removing the cooker from heat and then allow a natural release of 5 minutes.

4. In a large bowl, add cold water.

5. Use the quick-release method to release any remaining pressure then open the cooker.

6. Using an oven mitt or tongs, transfer the hot eggs to the cold water and allow it to cool for 6 minutes.

Apple Cranberry Steel Cut Oats

Serves 6

Ingredients

2 ½ teaspoons vanilla

¼ teaspoon salt

½ cup maple syrup

½ teaspoon nutmeg

2 teaspoons cinnamon

1 ½ teaspoon fresh lemon juice

4 tablespoons butter/virgin coconut oil

1 ½ cups cranberries

4 apples, diced

3 ½ cups water

1 cup yogurt

2 cups milk

2 cups steel cut oats

Directions

1. Start by greasing the bottom of the Instant Pot's inner pot using 1 tbsp. butter or virgin coconut oil.

2. Soak all the ingredients in the Instant Pot apart from the maple syrup, vanilla, salt, and milk for about 30 minutes. Soak and leave overnight for a better mix.

3. Next, add in the salt and maple syrup and cook on "Porridge/
   Congee". Do not forget to close the valve.

4. Allow the pot to get to the correct pressure that should take about
   20 minutes. Once it reaches the correct pressure level, allow another
   20 minutes (default time) for it to cook.

5. Now stir in the vanilla and serve with the milk.

6. Enjoy

Chinese Steamed Eggs

Serves 1

Ingredients

 Pinch of garlic powder, salt, and pepper

 Pinch of sesame seeds

 Chopped scallions

 ½ cup cold water

 2 large eggs

Directions

1. Into a small bowl, mix together the 2 eggs and ½ cup cold water.

2. Add in the garlic powder, salt, pepper, sesame seeds, chopped scallions and stir well; then set aside.

3. Now pour a cup of water into the inner pot of the Instant Pot then place a steamer basket in the pot.

4. Place the bowl that has the egg mixture on the steamer basket and then close the lid tight.

5. Now select the "steam" function and let it cook for 5 minutes.

6. Once ready, the timer should go off. Serve with hot rice and enjoy.

Poached Eggs Over Spicy Potato Hash

Serves 2

Ingredients

   1 teaspoon taco seasoning

   1 tablespoon chopped cilantro

   ½ cup of diced onion

   1 sliced jalapeno pepper

   2 tablespoons bacon fat or grass fed butter

   2 tablespoons of cooked and chopped bacon

   2 eggs

   1 cup of peeled and cubed potatoes

Directions

1. Into the inner pot of the pressure cooker, pour a cup of water and then place a trivet inside.

2. Place the cubed potatoes into a bowl then onto the trivet and close the lid tight as well as the vent valve.

3. Set the cooker to "Manual" and choose "High" pressure for 2 minutes to soften the potatoes.

4. Once done, press cancel and then remove the potatoes and set them aside.

5. Remove the trivet and drain the water. Set the pressure cooker to "Sauté" and "Adjust" for "more browning."

6. Add the 2 tbsp. butter or bacon fat and sauté the ½ cup of diced onions until they are radiant.

7. Then add in the pepper, bacon, cilantro, potatoes, and the taco seasoning and mix well. This should take about 5 minutes, remove when finished and place into a small bowl.

8. Ensure that you pat down the potatoes in order to create a little crater in the middle, and then place the bowl back into the Instant Pot.

9. Crack the eggs gently into the crater you've made into the potato hash; and now close the lid and vent valve.

10. Choose "Manual" and set the pressure to high and cook 2 minutes until the eggs become well poached.

11. Lift the potato hash with the eggs on top using a flat wooden spatula or other flexible spatula but be careful not to break the egg yolk.

12. Put the eggs and potato hash on a plate and then enjoy.

Apple Oatmeal Crisp

Serves 2

Ingredients

2 ½ cups water

1/3 cup melted butter

½ teaspoon salt

1 teaspoon cinnamon

½ cup brown sugar

1/3 cup flour

1 cup quick cooking oats

1 tablespoon lemon juice

4 cups apples, peeled, sliced and diced

Directions

1. Sprinkle the lemon juice on the apples

2. Combine and mix well the oats, salt, margarine, brown sugar, flour and cinnamon.

3. Arrange alternating layers of the oat and apple mixture in a buttered bowl that will fit into the Instant Pot. Now cover the bowl with aluminum foil.

4. Place a wire rack inside the pot then add water

5. Position the bowl on the rack inside the cooker.

6. Secure the lid

7. Now choose the "Porridge/Congee" function and "Adjust" for the extra time of 30 minutes.

8. Do a natural release of 15 minutes, then a quick release to get rid of any remaining pressure, and enjoy!

Clam Chowder

Serves 8

Ingredients

¼ cup butter

1 quart light cream

2 (8-ounce) cans minced clams

2 cups water

½ teaspoon pepper

2 teaspoons salt

4 cups cubed potatoes

2 cups chopped onions

4 slices bacon, chopped

Directions

1. Sauté onions and bacon into the pot using the "Sauté" function and just leave the heat on default for about 6 minutes.

2. Then add the pepper, water, potatoes, and salt. Now seal the lid completely.

3. Cook for about 5 minutes using the "Manual" setting.

4. Allow the pressure to be released naturally for 10 minutes, and then open carefully.

5. Drain the clams then add them slowly followed by ¼ cup butter, 1 quart light cream and 1 cup of clam liquid (from the cans), stirring thoroughly.

6. Allow everything then to simmer for 10 minutes using the "Sauté" function.

7. Serve and enjoy

Cinnamon Raisin Bread With Sauce

Serves 4

Ingredients

½ cup raisins

7 (¾ inch) thick sliced cinnamon bread, cubed and toasted

¼ teaspoon salt

½ teaspoon cinnamon, ground

2 teaspoon vanilla extract

4 eggs, beaten

3 cups whole milk

½ cup packed brown sugar

5 tablespoons butter, melted

Caramel Pecan Sauce

½ cup pecans, toasted and chopped

2 teaspoon vanilla extract

½ teaspoon salt

2 tablespoons butter

3 tablespoons cream

¼ cup corn syrup

¾ cup brown sugar

Directions

1. Stir together the 2 tbsp. vanilla, 4 beaten eggs, ¼ tbsp. salt, ½ tbsp. cinnamon, 3 cups milk, ½ cup sugar and 5 tbsp. melted butter in a large bowl.

2. Mix in the raisins and cubed bread and allow them to rest for approximately 2o minutes in order for the bread to absorb the liquid mix. Remember to stir regularly.

3. Into a metal baking dish (ensure this dish can fit into the inner pot), pour in the bread pudding and then cover the dish with foil.

4. Make a foil sling that should help you lift the dish from the cooker using an 18-inch foil folded lengthwise twice.

5. Into the Instant Pot, pour 1 ½ cups of water and fit the trivet in the bottom. Next, center the dish onto a foil strip and drop it carefully into the cooker.

6. Lock the lid and cook for 20 minutes over high pressure using the "Manual" setting.

7. Turn off the pressure cooker and perform a quick release. Wait for the valve to drop before you remove the lid.

8. Now remove the dish from the cooker and then position in a preheated 345 degrees oven to crisp up the top for 5-10 minutes.

9. To prepare the caramel pecan sauce, just mix together the butter, heavy cream, corn syrup, brown sugar and salt into the Instant Pot and "Sauté" them until the sauce melts.

10. Then lower the heat and simmer to ensure that all the sugar is dissolved and the sauce is smooth.

11. Now stir in the chopped pecans and the vanilla.

Blueberry And Banana Steel Cut Oats

Serves 2 - 3

Ingredients

Pinch of salt

1 tablespoon oil

2 cups water

½ cup steel cut oats

½ cup milk

¼ cup of granola or chopped nuts

½ cup of fresh or dried blueberries and bananas

¼ cup of agave syrup, maple syrup, brown or white sugar

Directions

1. Into the Instant Pot, combine all the ingredients minus the fruits and sweetener, select "Manual" then "High Pressure" then set to cook for ten minutes.

2. After the ten minutes, use the natural pressure release for around 15 minutes. Let the valve drop and then open the lid.

3. Stir the oats and allow it to rest for a minute in order to absorb water.

4. Now top with fresh or dried blueberries and bananas.

5. You can add any sweetener you prefer such as agave syrup, maple syrup, brown or white sugar.

6. Serve and enjoy

Buffalo Chicken Soup

Serves 4

Ingredients

4 chicken breasts, boneless and shredded

5 cups chicken broth

2 celery sticks, diced

½ onion, diced

2 cloves garlic, diced

3 tablespoons ranch

3 tablespoons butter

1 cup buffalo hot sauce

4 cups cheddar cheese, shredded

2 cups heavy cream

Directions

1. Into the Instant Pot, put all the ingredients except for the cream and cheese

2. Select the "Soup" function and "Adjust" down to 20 minutes.

3. Add in the cheese and heavy cream, then stir.

4. Enjoy

Onion Soup

Serves 4

Ingredients

   2 tablespoons coconut oil

   4 onions, diced

   2 tablespoons balsamic vinegar

   6 cups pork stock

   2 tablespoons salt

Directions

1. Into the Instant Pot, put all the ingredients in and stir well.

2. Select the "Soup" function and allow the default time of 30 minutes.

3. Natural release for 15 minutes, then enjoy.

Mexican Chicken Soup

Serves 6

Ingredients

- 1 tablespoon olive oil
- 1 ½ onion, diced
- 1 green pepper, diced
- 1 red pepper, diced
- 3 carrots, diced
- 2 cloves garlic, minced
- 5 chicken breasts, shredded
- 2 tomatoes, diced
- 4 tablespoons chili powder
- 2 tablespoons cumin
- 1 tablespoon paprika, smoked
- 1 tablespoon pepper
- 1 tablespoon salt
- ½ lime, juice squeezed
- 1 (10 oz) can tomato paste

Directions

1. Into the Instant Pot, add in the onion, peppers, carrots, and garlic. Select the "Sauté" function and cook for 5 minutes.

2. Add in the rest of the ingredients then stir thoroughly. Follow this by selecting the "Soup" function and use the default time of 30 minutes.

3. Do a natural release of 15 minutes.

4. Serve and enjoy.

Lunch Recipes

Cilantro Lime Rice

Serves 2

Ingredients

  3 tablespoons fresh cilantro, chopped

  1 tablespoon lime juice

  1 teaspoon salt

  2 tablespoons vegetable oil

  1 ¼ cups water

  1 cup long grain white rice

Directions

1. Into the Instant Pot, add in the rice, 1 tablespoon of vegetable oil and the water. Stir well.

2. Now lock the lid in place and cook at "manual" and "high pressure" for 3 minutes.

3. Once done, turn off the pressure cooker and do a natural release for 7 minutes. Follow this with a quick release to get rid of any remaining pressure.

4. Use a fork to fluff the rice.

5. Now mix 1 teaspoon of salt, 1 tablespoon of vegetable oil, 1 tablespoon of lime juice and 3 tablespoons of fresh chopped cilantro into a bowl.

6. Add the rice into the bowl and carefully mix all the ingredients together.

Collard Greens with Bacon

Serves 4

Ingredients

- 1 teaspoon sugar

- ½ teaspoon salt

- 1 tablespoon balsamic vinegar

- 4 minced garlic cloves

- 1 onion, sliced and diced

- 2 tablespoons diced tomatoes or 2 tablespoons tomato puree

- 2 tablespoons olive oil

- ½ cup chicken broth

- 1 bunch fresh collard greens

- 4 bacon strips

Directions

1. Wash and clean the collard greens thoroughly. It is recommended you soak them into cold water for about 30 minutes.

2. Mix the tomato puree/diced tomatoes, garlic, chicken broth, vinegar, oil and onion into the Instant Pot and then stir thoroughly to combine all the ingredients.

3. Remove the soaked greens from the water one by one ensuring that you don't disturb the water to keep dirt at the bottom while the collard greens float.

4. Chop the collard greens into small pieces of about an inch.

5. Mix the greens with salt and sugar and then add them to the pot, to coat with the oil mixture.

6. Chop the bacon strips into small pieces and add to the pot

7. Cook in the Instant Pot on "Manual" and "High Pressure" for 20 minutes.

Chili Salad

Serves 6

Ingredients

2 cups water

½ teaspoon kosher salt

2 teaspoons ground cumin

3 tablespoons chili powder

½ teaspoon crushed red pepper flakes

2 teaspoons unsweetened cocoa powder

1 tablespoon dark brown sugar

4 tablespoons tomato paste

2 (15 ounce) cans diced tomatoes, un-drained

2 (15 ounce) cans dark red kidney beans, rinsed and drained

3 cloves garlic, minced

1 jalapeno pepper, seeded and chopped

1 small green bell pepper, chopped

1 sweet onion, slice and diced

2 teaspoons olive oil

1.5 pounds ground beef

Directions

1. Place the ground beef into the Instant Pot. Select "Meat" and "Adjust" for 20 minutes until it becomes crumbly and brown. Remove the ground beef and drain off any excess fat.

2. Pour in the olive oil to the pressure cooker and stir in the green pepper, jalapeno pepper and onion. Choose the "Sauté " feature and cook for 6 minutes.

3. After 6 minutes add garlic and cook for 2 more minutes.

4. Return the meat to the cooker, and mix in the tomatoes, brown sugar, kidney beans, chili powder, salt, red pepper flakes, tomato paste, water, cumin, and cocoa powder.

5. Lock the lid, choose "Manual" and under "High Pressure", cook for about 10 minutes.

6. Allow 5 to 10 minutes for a natural release.

7. Stir the chili after the pressure is released and serve.

Braised Kale and Carrots

Serves 2

Ingredients

¼ teaspoon red pepper flakes

A pinch of kosher salt

½ cup chicken broth

4 cloves of garlic, peeled and chopped

3 medium carrots, diced

1 medium onion, diced

1 tablespoon of ghee

10 ounces of kale, chopped

1 tablespoon aged balsamic vinegar

Pepper, freshly ground

Ingredients

1. Into the Instant Pot, melt 1 tablespoon of ghee using the "Sauté" function; this should take about 3-4 minutes.

2. Toss in the chopped onions and carrots and again, choose "Sauté" and continue until they are well softened. This should take about 6-8 minutes.

3. Add in the garlic and continue to stir for about 2 minutes.

4. Next, add in the kales, followed by the chicken broth then sprinkle a pinch of kosher salt and pepper.

5. Lock the lid and select "Manual" and "High Pressure", and cook for 10 minutes.

6. Once done, allow the pressure to release naturally for about 10-15 minutes. Alternately, you can try the quick release method if you're hungry and cannot wait.

7. Remove the lid, swirl everything to get a good mix.

8. Add red pepper flakes and 1 tbsp. balsamic vinegar.

9. Serve and enjoy.

Pot Roast

Serves 5-7

Ingredients

½ cup cold water

3 onions, peeled and diced

8 potatoes, peeled and halved

2 ½ cups cold water

2 (1.5 ounce) packages dry onion soup mix

¼ cup vegetable shortening

1/3 cup all-purpose flour

Salt and ground black pepper

3 pounds beef rump roast

Directions

1. Start by seasoning the rump roast with pepper, salt and then coat with flour. Reserve any leftover flour for use in making the gravy.

2. In the Instant Pot, melt the vegetable shortening using "Sauté", and then add the rump roast and brown on all sides.

3. Sprinkle the dry onion soup mix on the roast, and then pour about 2 cups of water.

4. Now close the lid and select "Manual", and "High Pressure." Cook for 2 hours.

5. Do a quick release then add onions and potatoes, ensuring the vegetables are inside the cooking liquid. You can position the rump roast on the vegetables or add more water to submerge the vegetables.

6. Lock the lid and return to "Manual" and "High pressure." Cook for 15 minutes before releasing the pressure.

7. Transfer the vegetables and meat to a serving plate.

8. Bring the cooking liquid to a boil to make gravy. Whisk the reserved flour in ½-cup cold water.

9. Into the boiling broth, add in the flour mixture and cook until it has thickened enough. You can use the "Sauté" function here, ensuring to stir after every 2-4 minutes.

10. Serve the gravy with the hot vegetables and pot roast.

Split Pea and Ham Soup

Serves 6-8

Ingredients

- 1 ½ teaspoons dried thyme
- 3 celery ribs, diced
- 2 carrots, diced
- 1 onion, diced
- 2 pounds of ham, chunks
- 8 cups water
- 1 pound of dried split peas
- ¼ cup Sherry wine

Directions

1. Put all the ingredients except the sherry wine in the Instant Pot and fill half the cooker with water.

2. Lock the lid

3. Bring the contents to high pressure using the "Manual" and "High Pressure" settings. Set for about 20 minutes.

4. Once finished, do a natural release of 10-15 minutes.

5. Season and serve with Sherry wine.

Chicken Stock

Serves 8

Ingredients

    1 teaspoon sea salt

    4 quarts cold water

    14 whole black peppercorns

    8 cloves garlic

    1 leftover chicken carcass

    1 large carrot, cut into 4 pieces

    1 large onion, quartered

    1 stalk celery, quartered

Directions

1. Place the peppercorns, garlic cloves, chicken carcass, celery, carrot, and onion in the Instant Pot.

2. Add water to two-third fullness, and then secure the lid.

3. Bring the pressure cooker to high pressure using the "Manual" and "High Pressure" settings. Cook for 30 minutes.

4. After half an hour, allow 10-15 minutes for a natural release of pressure. Do not use a quick-release method in this situation.

5. Remove the lid then strain the stock into a different bowl and discard the vegetables and chicken bones.

6. Let the mixture cool at room temperature before you transfer to the fridge.

7. Once cooled, the fat will rise to the surface and solidify. You can then skim the fat off completely then season with sea salt. Serve this with your favorite bread.

Potato Salad

Serves 8

Ingredients

1 teaspoon cider vinegar

2 teaspoon yellow mustard

1 cup mayonnaise

2 tablespoon chopped fresh dill

5 hard-cooked eggs, chopped

Salt and pepper

2 stalk celery, chopped

½ cup chopped onion

1 cup water

8 potatoes

Directions

1. Peel the potatoes then place them into the Instant Pot with water and cook for about 3-4 minutes at "High Pressure" using the "Manual" setting.

2. Allow a natural release of 10 minutes, and then perform a quick release to get rid of excess pressure.

3. When the potatoes are cool enough, dice them.

4. Into a large bowl, alternate layers of onion, celery and potatoes and season each layer with pepper and salt.

5. Add in the chopped eggs to top up and then sprinkle with dill.

6. Mix mustard, cider vinegar and mayonnaise in a bowl before gently stirring the mayonnaise mixture into the potatoes.

7. Allow a chill time of approximately an hour before serving the salad.

Yogurt and Barley Soup

Serves 6

Ingredients

Salt and ground pepper

3 tablespoons chopped fresh mint

800 ml plain yogurt, lightly beaten

1.5 liters chicken stock

4 tablespoons pearl barley, rinsed

150 g finely chopped onion

2 tablespoons butter

Directions

1. Heat the butter in the pressure cooker and "Sauté" the onion until it has wilted for about 1 minute, before adding the stock and barley. Cook for 5 minutes.

2. Secure the lid and bring the cooker and cook for 15 minutes using the "Manual" setting.

3. Release the pressure naturally for about 10 minutes, and allow the contents to cool before transferring to another container and storing it in the fridge.

4. Later, stir in the yogurt and add the mint.

5. Season with pepper and salt to taste.

6. Garnish with the remaining mint and serve it cold.

Red Beans and Sausages

Serves: 8-10

Ingredients

> 5 cups of water
>
> ½ teaspoon cumin
>
> 1 teaspoon parsley, dried
>
> 2 teaspoon salt
>
> 1 green bell pepper, diced
>
> 1 stalk celery, quartered
>
> ½ onion, diced
>
> ½ glove garlic, diced
>
> 2 tablespoons Cajun
>
> 2 bay leaves
>
> 2 pounds smoked sausage, sliced thinly
>
> 1.5 pound dried red beans, thoroughly rinsed

Directions

1. Combine all ingredients into the Instant Pot. (Be wary to not go over the safety line, inside the pot)
2. Seal the lid and select "Bean/Chili" and cook on its default setting.
3. Once finished, allow 15-20 minutes for a natural release, then serve and enjoy.

Asian Pepper Steak

Serves 4

Ingredients

 3 tablespoons potato starch or cornstarch

 2 tablespoons water

 ¼ cup soy sauce

 5 green onions, coarsely chopped

 1 green bell pepper, diced

 2 tomatoes, diced

 ½ teaspoon red pepper flakes

 1 teaspoon ginger root, grated

 ½ teaspoon salt

 1 teaspoon light brown sugar

 2 tablespoon Sherry

 ½ cup beef broth

 1 pound beef round steak, cut into 3 inch pieces

 2 cloves garlic, diced

 1 large onion, diced

 3 tablespoons olive oil

 2 tablespoon sesame oil

 Basmati rice, cooked

Directions

1. Heat the olive and sesame oils in the pressure cooker, then add garlic and onion, then select "Sauté" and cook for about 4 minutes.

2. Add the beef strips while continuously stirring and cooking the contents for 2 minutes using "Sauté".

3. Stir in the pepper flakes, ginger root, salt, brown sugar, sherry and the broth. Next secure the lid.

4. Select "Poultry" and just use the default time of 15 minutes. Once finished, release the pressure with either a 15 minute natural release or a quick release.

5. Stir in the green onions, tomatoes and bell pepper and secure the lid. Next, cook under "Manual" and "High Pressure" for 2 minutes.

6. Release the pressure naturally for 10 minutes then remove the lid.

7. Mix potato starch, water and soy sauce in a small bowl until smooth.

8. Add the beef and veggies, stirring slowly until it thickens and becomes creamy.

9. Serve the vegetable and beef with the rice and enjoy.

Ratatouille Vegetable Stew

Serves 4

Ingredients

¼ cup chicken or vegetable stock

3 tablespoons minced parsley

2 medium tomatoes, diced

2 cloves garlic, minced

1 large onion, diced

2 green peppers, seeded and cut into 1 inch slices

1 medium potato, diced

2 medium zucchini, cut into ½ inch slices

1 small eggplant peeled and cut in 1-inch cubes

4 tablespoons canola or olive oil

Directions

1. Into the Instant Pot, heat half of the olive oil then stir fry the potato, zucchini, and eggplant. Use the "Sauté" feature, this should take about 6-8 minutes then remove the contents onto a serving dish.

2. Add the garlic and onion and "Sauté" to soften the onion, this should take about 4 minutes.

3. Put the vegetables back into to the cooker together with the remaining ingredients, and then secure the lid.

4. Select "Manual" and "High Pressure" then cook for 6-8 minutes. Follow this with a natural release for 10 minutes.

5. To completely dry the stew, simmer the contents while open for a few minutes.

Beef Bourguignon

Serves 4

Ingredients

800 grams steak, diced into 1 inch pieces.

½ cup beef stock

2 carrots, diced

4 bacon, diced

2 tablespoons flour

½ onion, diced

½ tablespoons basil

1 clove garlic, minced

Directions

1. Into the Instant Pot, add the bacon, onion, and steak. Select "Manual" and "High Pressure", and then set the timer for 10 minutes.

2. Natural Release, then stir in the flour thoroughly

3. Add in the rest of the ingredients.

4. Select "Meat/Stew" and allow the default time of 35 minutes to cook".

5. Do a quick release, then serve and enjoy.

Mexican Beef Stew

Serves 4

Ingredients

2 tablespoons coconut oil

2 onions, diced

3 pounds beef, sliced into 1 inch pieces

3 teaspoons salt

2 teaspoons cumin

2 teaspoons paprika, smoked

2 teaspoons oregano, dried

1 teaspoon pepper

2 teaspoons chipotle powder

2 cups bone broth

1 tomato, diced

Directions

1. Into the Instant Pot, put all the ingredients in and stir well.

2. Select the "Soup" function and allow the default time of 30 minutes.

3. Natural release for 15 minutes, then enjoy.

Dinner Recipes

—————— ❖ ——————

Spaghetti and Spaghetti Sauce

Serves 6

Ingredients

> 6 cups hot cooked spaghetti
>
> 6-ounce can tomato paste
>
> 28-ounce can stew tomatoes
>
> 1 bay leaf
>
> ½ teaspoon crushed red pepper
>
> 1 teaspoon dried oregano, crushed
>
> 1 teaspoon sugar
>
> 1/3 cup snipped fresh parsley
>
> 2 cloves garlic, minced
>
> ½ cup sliced celery
>
> ½ cup chopped onion
>
> 1 pound pork sausage or Italian sausage, cut into ½ inch slices
>
> ½ pound ground beef

Directions

1. Cook the sausage and beef in the Instant Pot. Use the "Meat" function and adjust to 20 minutes.

2. Do a quick release then drain the fat and return it to cooker.

3. Next add the tomato paste, stewed tomatoes, bay leaf, crushed red pepper, dried oregano, sugar, parsley, garlic, celery, and onions.

4. Lock the lid.

5. Select "Manual" and "High Pressure", then cook for 12 minutes.

6. Do a quick release then remove the lid carefully.

7. Remove the bay leaf and serve the sauce over spaghetti.

Whole chicken

Serves 6

Ingredients

1 tablespoon coconut oil

1 cup water

1 teaspoon garlic powder

1 teaspoon dry mustard powder

1 teaspoon black pepper

1 teaspoon onion powder

1 whole chicken

Directions

1. Into your Instant Pot, add a cup of water and then place a steam rack inside the instant pot.

2. Pour 1 tablespoon of coconut oil over the chicken then cover the chicken with the garlic powder, dry mustard powder, black pepper, and onion powder.

3. Place the chicken on the steam rack.

4. Now lock the lid and set the cooker to the "Poultry" setting and cook the chicken for the default time of 30 minutes.

5. Let the chicken sit in the pot for 15 minutes as the pressure releases naturally. Enjoy

6. Remember that the bones can be used to make bone broth so don't throw them away!

Chicken Soup

Serves 5-7

Ingredients

    1 cup mild salsa

    16 ounce fresh spinach leaves, diced

    15 ounce chickpeas, drained

    5 cups chicken stock

    ½ cup chopped parsley

    1 bone chicken breast half, skin removed

    1 cup green lentils

    ½ cup pearl barley

    2 cloves garlic, minced

    4 Italian turkey sausage, cut into thin slices

    3 teaspoons olive oil

    2 sliced medium onion

Directions

1. Heat 2 teaspoons of olive oil in your Instant Pot, then add the sausages. "Sauté" for 6-8 minutes until the sausages starts to brown.

2. Transfer the sausages to a plate and drain the oil, then add 1 teaspoon of olive oil to the pressure cooker.

3. "Sauté" the onion and garlic until the onion turns transparent which should take a minute, then add barley; stir frequently

4. Return the sausage to the pressure cooker and add parsley, lentils, chicken, and the chicken stock.

5. Secure the lid.

6. Select the "Soup" function and "Adjust" down to 20 minutes.

7. Allow a natural release of 15 minutes, then open the pressure cooker and remove the chicken breast with the bone. Shred the meat and return the meat to the soup.

8. Before serving, add salsa, spinach and garbanzo beans, and stir thoroughly.

Hearty Pot Roast

Serves 8

Ingredients

5 large potatoes, peeled and cut into bite-size pieces

3 carrots, peeled and cut into bite-size pieces

1 large onion, cut into 4 slices

1 ½ tablespoons Worcestershire sauce

1 (14.5 ounce) can beef broth

2 pinch onion powder

2 pinch seasoned salt

Ground black pepper

1 (3 pound) boneless beef chuck roast, trimmed

2 tablespoons vegetable oil

Directions

1. Heat the 2 tbsp. vegetable oil in the Instant Pot using "Sauté" and brown the roast while seasoning with onion powder, pepper, and seasoned salt. Recommended cook time is 10 minutes.

2. Pour in the Worcestershire sauce and the beef broth, followed by the 4 slices of onion.

3. Seal the lid and select the "Meat/Stew" function; use the default time of 35 minutes. Once finished, use the quick release method to release the pressure.

4. Mix in the potatoes and the carrots and seal the lid again.

5. Select the "Meat/Stew" function again but "Adjust" it down to 20 minutes.

6. Use the quick release method to release the inside pressure, and then serve the vegetables and the roast to a dish.

7. Enjoy

Lentils with Chorizo Sausage

Serves 2-3

Ingredients

Pinch of salt

1 bay leaf

1 teaspoon paprika

1 liter cold water

3 garlic cloves, minced

1 medium onion, diced

1 large carrot, peeled

150 g chorizo sausage

225 g brown lentils

Directions

1. Put the lentils, peeled carrot, diced onion, minced garlic cloves and bay leaf into the Instant Pot.

2. Chop the chorizo into 6 pieces and put it in the cooker followed by cold water, paprika and a pinch of salt.

3. Seal the lid

4. Use the "Bean/Chili" function and "Adjust" for 25 minutes. Then use a natural release of 15 minutes.

5. Finally, stir well then enjoy.

Pork Tenderloin

Serves 6

Ingredients

¼ cup lemon juice

1 cup chicken broth

1 ½ pound pork tenderloin

¼ teaspoon salt

½ teaspoon red pepper flakes

2 cloves garlic, minced

¼ cup lime juice

¼ cup olive oil

¼ cup fresh cilantro leaves

Directions

1. "Sauté" the red pepper flakes, garlic, lime juice, olive oil, cilantro and salt for about 6 minutes.

2. For maximum flavor, add the marinade into a sealable container then put the tenderloins in as well and refrigerate for 8 hours.

3. In the bottom of a pressure cooker, stir lemon juice and chicken broth together and lay the tenderloin into the pressure cooker ensuring it is submerged in the liquid.

4. Pour any remaining marinade over the tenderloin.

5. Select the "Meat/Stew" function and cook for the default time of 35 minutes.

6. Do a natural release for 20 minutes.

7. You can slice the tenderloin into medallions when serving.

Southern Red Beans & Rice Stew

Serves 8

Ingredients

6 cups water

1 lb. dried red kidney beans

1 teaspoon liquid smoke

2 tablespoon Worcestershire sauce

1 bay leaf

1 teaspoon dried thyme

¼ teaspoon fresh ground pepper

½ teaspoon cayenne pepper

3 teaspoons kosher salt

3 tablespoons garlic, chopped

½ cup celery, chopped

1 bell pepper, chopped

1 ½ cups onions, chopped

3 tablespoons olive oil

Directions

1. Heat olive oil using the "Sauté" function for about 2 minutes.

2. Then "Sauté" in the celery, garlic, bell pepper and the onions for 5 minutes.

3. Add the remaining ingredients then secure the lid.

4. Select "Stew" and "Adjust" up to 45 minutes.

5. Allow a natural release for 15 minutes.

6. Remove the lid after the cooker has cooled, and use a slotted spoon to remove the bay leaves.

7. Now you can smash the beans using a potato masher, then stir into the stew for 5 minutes to allow the stew to thicken.

8. If necessary, add water or adjust seasoning to taste. Serve the stew over hot cooked rice.

Chuck Roast

Serves 6

Ingredients

  14.5 ounce beef broth

  1.5 ounce package brown gravy mix

  1 ounce package dry ranch style dressing mix

  1 ounce package Italian salad dressing mix

  1 large onion, sliced

  3 pounds beef chuck roast

  2 tablespoons oil

Directions

1. Select "Sauté" then add 2 tbsp. oil, heat for 3 minutes then add the beef chuck roast in and brown for 10 minutes using the "Sauté" function.

2. Mix the gravy mix, Italian salad dressing mix and ranch dressing mix in a bowl or cup. Sprinkle the dressings over the browned roast.

3. Once done, pour the beef broth into the pressure cooker followed by chopped onion. Put the lid and lock the pressure cooker.

4. Select "Meat/Stew" and "Adjust" up to 45 minutes.

5. Allow a natural release of 15 minutes.

6. You can thicken the juices with flour or cornstarch for making gravy.

7. Enjoy

Chicken with Duck Sauce

Serves 4

Ingredients

¼ cup chicken broth

½ teaspoon dried marjoram

½ teaspoon paprika

Salt and pepper

3 pound whole chicken, cut into small pieces

1 tablespoon olive oil

Duck Sauce:

2 tablespoons honey

1 ½ teaspoons minced fresh ginger root

2 tablespoons white vinegar

¼ cup apricot preserves

Directions

1. Select "Sauté" and cook the olive oil for 3 minutes.

2. Add the chicken and brown on all the sides, using the "Sauté" feature, this should take about 8-10 minutes.

3. Season the chicken with dried marjoram, salt, pepper and paprika, and then drain and discard the fat from the cooker.

4. Mix in chicken broth then seal the lid.

5. Select "Poultry" and "Adjust" for 30 minutes.

6. To serve the dish, remove the chicken to a serving dish and add vinegar, honey, apricot leaves, and ginger to the pot.

7. Boil and cook the mixture up to when a thick syrupy substance has been formed. The cook time is approximately 10 minutes and you can simply use the "Sauté" function.

8. Spread the sauce over the chicken and then serve your dish.

Beef Stew

Serves 4

Ingredients

1 bay leaf

1 ½ teaspoons thyme

1 tablespoon brown sugar

2 tablespoons balsamic vinegar

3 tablespoons tomato paste

1 (14 ounce) cans tomatoes, un-drained

½ cup chopped carrot

3 cups diced potatoes

2 tablespoons minced garlic

½ cup chopped onion

½ cup beef broth

1 ½ teaspoons olive oil

1 lb. lean beef, cubed

¼ teaspoon dry mustard

½ teaspoon salt

¼ cup flour

Salt and pepper

Directions

1. In a plastic bag, mix the salt, flour and dry mustard. Once thoroughly mixed, add the beef and shake to coat.

2. "Sauté" oil in the Instant Pot for 3 minutes then empty the contents of the plastic bag into the pot. Brown the beef for 10 minutes using the "Sauté" feature.

3. Add the broth and remaining ingredients and lock the lid.

4. Select "Meat/Stew", and "Adjust" the time down to 20 minutes.

5. Do a quick release, remove the bay leaf, and enjoy.

Golden Mushroom Beef Stew

Serves 4

Ingredients

15 ounces water

10 ounces condensed golden mushroom soup

10 button mushrooms, rinsed and halved

2 teaspoons dried parsley

Salt & pepper

4 red potatoes cut into chunks

4 carrots, peeled and cut into chunks

1 large onion, cut up

1 ½ lbs. stew meat

2 tablespoons canola oil

1 - 2 beef bouillon cubes

Directions

1. Add oil into the pot and "Sauté" for 3 minutes. Next, continuing the "Sauté" function, sear the stew meat on all sides, this will take approximately 6 minutes.

2. Next, add the carrots, salt, onions, parsley, water, beef bouillon cubes, potatoes, mushrooms, pepper and golden mushroom soup. Stir well.

3. Close the lid of the cooker.

4. Select the "Meat/Stew" function and set it for the default time of 35 minutes.

5. Allow a natural release of 15 minutes.

6. To make the stew thicker, stir 1 tbsp. cornstarch with ½ cup water and add them to the stew. Select "Sauté" and "Adjust" for the simmer feature, then cook for 5 minutes or until the stew thickens.

7. Enjoy

Cajon Sausage Risotto

Serves 4

Ingredients

- 2 pounds sausage meat, sliced
- 2 tablespoons Cajun
- 2 teaspoons salt
- 5 tablespoons butter
- 2 cups rice
- 3 cups chicken stock
- 2 bell peppers, seeded and diced
- 2 cups green onion, diced

Directions

1. Add butter into the Instant Pot and "Sauté" for 3 minutes until melted.

2. Add in the sliced sausages and continue to "Sauté" for another 3 minutes until the sausages are brown.

3. Add in the rest of the ingredients

4. Select the "Multigrain" function, and allow the default time of 40 minutes to cook.

5. Natural release for 15 minutes.

6. Serve and enjoy.

Buffalo Chicken With Sweet Potatoes

Serves 4

Ingredients

3 pounds chicken breast, sliced into 1 inch pieces

1 onion, diced

5 tablespoons butter

5 tablespoons buffalo sauce

18 ounces sweet potatoes, diced

1 teaspoon onion powder

1 teaspoon garlic powder

1 teaspoon salt

1 teaspoon pepper

Directions

1. Add the onion and butter into the Instant Pot and "Sauté" for 3 minutes until browned and melted, respectively.

2. Add in the rest of the ingredients and mix thoroughly.

3. Close the lid and select the "Poultry" function and "Adjust" up to 30 minutes.

4. Allow 15 minutes for a natural release.

5. Serve and enjoy.

Lemon Curry Rice

Serves 4

Ingredients

- 1 can coconut milk
- ½ lemon, juice squeezed
- 2 tablespoons curry powder
- 1 tablespoon salt
- 1 tablespoon turmeric
- 3 pounds chicken, breast or thighs, shredded
- 4 bowls rice, cooked

Directions

1. Add all the ingredients into the Instant Pot and stir thoroughly
2. Select the "Poultry" function and "Adjust" up to 30 minutes.
3. Do a quick release
4. Serve over the rice and enjoy

Dessert Recipes

———— ❖ ————

Condensed Milk Dulce De Leche

Yields: 1 can

Ingredients

Water

1 can of condensed milk, sweetened

Directions

1. Into the Instant Pot, put a trivet and then position a can of condensed milk firmly. Ensure that it doesn't touch the side or the base of your cooker.

2. Add water in order to cover the can until it is submerged. (It is very important that the can becomes completely submerged)

3. Now lock the lid.

4. Choose the "Soup" function and "Adjust" up to 40 minutes.

5. Carefully do a quick release. Use tongs or some other handy kitchen utensil to take the can out.

6. Place the can on a heatproof surface in room temperature.

7. Once the can cools, enjoy!

** You can keep the dulce de leche in the fridge for 3 weeks only if it's in airtight bag/container/original unopened can.

Cinnamon-Flavored Stewed Fruits

Serves: 6

Ingredients

1 cinnamon stick

¾ cup packed brown sugar

1 cup water

1 cup red wine

2 lemon slices

1 lb. mixed dried fruits prunes, figs, apples

Whipped cream (optional)

Directions

1. Toss and mix the lemon slices, cinnamon stick, sugar, water, and wine into the Instant Pot.

2. Bring the mixture to a boil using the "Sauté" function for 6-8 minutes, then allow for it to simmer for another 3-5 minutes until the sugar completely dissolves, then add in the mixed fruits.

3. Now lock the lid in place and then bring the cooker to pressure using "Manual" and "High Pressure, for 6 minutes.

4. Once done, release the pressure. You can then either serve it either chilled or warm, alongside whipped cream if you desire.

Banana Pudding

Serves 4

Ingredients

    2 cups water

    1 teaspoon pure vanilla extract

    1 ½ teaspoons dark rum

    ½ cup sour cream

    ½ cup sweetened condensed milk

    ½ cup half-and-half

    4 tablespoons sugar

    2 large egg yolks

    1 medium very ripe banana

    1 large egg

Directions

1. Puree the banana in a blender or food processor.

2. Mix the condensed milk, rum, eggs, half-and-half, vanilla, and sour cream. Then strain the mixture through a fine strainer.

3. Transfer the mixture to 6 oz. soufflé dishes then cover tightly with aluminum foil.

4. Add 2 cups of water to the cooker.

5. Insert a steamer basket into the Instant Pot then add the soufflé dishes ensuring that the water cannot reach the steamer. (Can use a trivet for extra precaution)

6. Seal the cooker

7. Select "Manual" and "High Pressure", and cook for 8 minutes.

8. Let the pressure naturally release for 15 minutes.

9. Remove the dishes and refrigerate them for 2 days while covered.

Hazelnut Flan

Serves 8

Ingredients

For the Custard:

> 3 tablespoons Hazelnut syrup
>
> ½ cup whipping cream
>
> 2 teaspoons vanilla extract
>
> 2 cups whole milk
>
> Pinch of salt
>
> 2/3 cup granulated sugar
>
> 2 egg yolks
>
> 3 whole eggs

For the Caramel:

> 1 cup granulated sugar
>
> ¼ cup water

Directions

1. To prepare the caramel, add ¼ cup water and 1 cup sugar to a saucepan. Cover and let the contents boil over medium heat for 2 minutes to allow sugar crystals to dissolve.

2. Remove the lid and cook uncovered until amber, but do not stir. To keep the mixture moving, swirl the pan gently before it turns too dark.

3. Pour into 8 (6 ounces) ungreased custard cups and set aside.

4. Whisk the eggs and yolks in a large bowl with 2/3 cup sugar plus some salt. Heat milk in a saucepan until it starts bubbling on medium heat.

5. Add the hot milk gradually to the eggs to temper them, before whisking in hazelnut syrup, cream and vanilla.

6. In a large measuring bowl, strain the contents. Then measure 1 ½ cups water and add to the Instant Pot, while placing a trivet at the bottom.

7. Into custard cup lined with caramel, pour in the custard and cover with foil and then place on trivet in the cooker. You should stack the cups in a second layer.

8. Secure the lid and cook for 6 minutes using "Manual" and "High Pressure" until a beep sounds.

9. When the beep sounds, turn off the pressure cooker and do a quick release for any accumulated pressure then remove the lid.

10. Remove carefully the cups into a wire rack and allow it to cool uncovered. After cooling, refrigerate the contents for about 4 hours while covered with plastic wrap.

11. To serve, run a knife around the ramekins, hold a plate on top then flip over.

12. Top the flan with whipped cream.

Creamy Rice Pudding

Serves 6

Ingredients

    1 cup raisins

    2 teaspoons vanilla extract

    1 cup half and half

    2 eggs

    5 cups milk

    ½ teaspoon salt

    1 cup sugar

    1 ½ cups Arborio rice

Directions

1. Mix together milk, salt, sugar and rice in the Instant Pot and then select the "Sauté" function.

2. Bring the mixture to a boil, which should take about 6-8 minutes, ensuring that you stir frequently to dissolve the sugar. One the mixture boils, lock the lid in place. Select "Manual" and "Low Pressure" and set the timer to 15 minutes.

3. As the rice cooks, whisk the eggs alongside the vanilla extract and half-and-half.

4. After the 15 minutes are over, turn off the pressure cooker, let the cooker natural release for 15 minutes then do a quick release to get rid of any excess pressure.

5. Remove the lid carefully and stir the rice in the pot, and then stir in the eggs into the pot and select the "Sauté" setting.

6. Cook the rice uncovered until the mixture starts to boil, which should take 8-10 minutes, then turn off the cooker and stir in the raisins.

7. Serve the pudding instantly or pour into serving dishes to cool down. As it cools, the pudding should thicken, and then if you want, you can add some more half and half.

8. If desired serve it cold with a sprinkle of cinnamon on top!

Cheesecake

Serves 2

Ingredients

   5 tablespoons melted butter

   Pinch of salt

   2 teaspoon of sugar

   1 cup butter cookie crumbs

Directions

1. To prepare the crust, process the butter cookie crumbs in a food processor.

2. Add in a pinch of salt and the melted butter so that the crumbs resemble wet sand and can hold together when pressed.

3. Place a parchment paper on a buttered removable pan disc, and then butter sides of pan.

4. Press the mixture evenly onto the pan's bottom and then up the sides of the pan slightly with a small round.

For Filling

   Grated lemon rind

   3 teaspoon vanilla

   3 eggs

   1 cup sugar

   2 tablespoons sour cream

¼ teaspoon salt

2 (8oz) softened cream cheese

Directions

1. Process the cheese in a food processor for 30 seconds and then add in sour cream and salt. Add in the sugar and process once more.

2. Now add in the eggs, each at a time and process with each addition. Follow each time with a teaspoon of vanilla.

3. Scrape down the bowl as you mix the filling in the processor and continue to process until it is smooth.

4. Now pour into the waiting pan that is lined with the crust and cover using folded paper towel. Also secure the paper towel with the foil.

5. Add 2 cups of water into the Instant Pot and place a trivet in the pot alongside the foil sling.

6. Lower the pan already centered on the sling. You should ensure that you leave space around the sides of the pan in order for the steam to rise.

7. Cook for 40 minutes using "Manual" and "High pressure", and then do natural pressure release. Now lift the cake out using the sling handle and position on the rack to cool.

8. In case you find any water on your cake, you can absorb it using the corner of the paper towel. You should now have a velvet textured cake without any cracks!

9. Now combine a cup of sour cream with sugar based on your preferences, with some salt and vanilla.

10. Once the cake has cooled down, cover it but leave the foil cocked in order for any trapped heat to escape. Then secure the foil tightly.

11. To serve, position the center of the removable bottom on a tall glass. Push down towards the glass gently in order to remove the sides of the pan but take care not to knock the glass over.

12. To separate the parchment from the cake, use a butcher's knife, and slide the cake onto the serving platter.

13. To slide cold , just run a knife under water, ensuring that you rinse and wipe the knife after each cut to ensure a perfect cut.

Chocolate Cake

Yields 6" cake

Ingredients

- 1 teaspoon of vanilla extract

- ½ teaspoon of vinegar or lemon juice

- 1/2 cup of milk

- ¼ cup of water

- 1 egg

- 1 cup of sugar

- 4 tablespoon of butter, softened

- 4 tablespoon of cocoa powder

- ¼ teaspoon of salt

- ¾ teaspoon of baking soda

- ¾ cup of plain flour

Directions

1. First whisk the flour, baking soda and salt in a bowl until it's well mixed then put it aside.

2. Then, again using the whisk, cream the sugar and butter in a separate bowl until it comes together.

3. Now add in the eggs and continue to beat until the mixture is somewhat fluffy. Add in cocoa and water and combine well for the cocoa to blend in fully.

4. Next, add in lemon juice or vinegar and the vanilla and continue to mix.

5. Follow this with the flour mixture in 2 additions, and ensure you fold gently after each addition. Try to mix until there are no more traces of flour that remain and the batter is lump free.

6. Now grease a small 6-inch pan using butter and then pour in the prepared batter. Then firmly tap the cake pan on the kitchen counter a number of times to remove the air bubbles from the batter.

7. Place the pan at the bottom of the pressure pan.

8. Heat the cooker using "Multigrain" for the default time of 40 minutes.

9. Once finished, do a quick release to get rid of the pressure.

10. Remove the cake from inside of the cooker and chill for around 10 minutes in a cake pan.

11. Place the cake gently on a plate or cooling rack for it to chill completely. Once done, just cut and serve. If you're looking to make a larger cake, feel free to use this cake as base and frost it and make multiple layers as you desire.

Crème Brulee

Serves 6

Ingredients

8 tablespoons superfine sugar

2 teaspoons vanilla

3 cups heavy cream

Pinch of salt

1/3 cup granulated sugar

8 egg yolks

Directions

1. Add 1 ½ cups of water into the Instant Pot, and then put a trivet at the bottom.

2. Whisk the eggs yolks, a pinch of salt and 1/3 cup of granulated sugar in a large mixing bowl. Then add in vanilla and cream and whisk until they are mixed well.

3. Into a large measuring bowl, strain the contents using a pitcher or a pour stout. Then pour the mixture into 6 custard cups and cover with aluminum foil.

4. Put the trivet in the Instant Pot and stack the cups into layers. If desired, you can use a second trivet in between the two layers.

5. Lock the lid and select "Manual" and "High Pressure", then cook for 8 minutes. After 8 minutes, turn off the cooker and release the pressure using a quick release.

6. Remove the cups carefully from the inner pot and transfer to a wire rack to cool while uncovered. Once cool, refrigerate when covered with a plastic wrap for 2-48 hours.

7. You can then sprinkle with a tablespoon of sugar over each curd's surface.

8. In a circular motion, use a long lighter and move the flame 2 inches above the surface in each curd in order to melt the sugar and create a crispy and caramelized top.

Pumpkin Pie

Serves 6 - 8

Ingredients

For Crust

    3 tablespoons butter melted

    1/3 cup toasted pecans, chopped

    6 crushed Pecan cookies

For filling

    ½ cup evaporated milk (unsweetened condensed milk)

    1 ½ cups solid pack pumpkin

    1 egg, beaten

    2 teaspoons pumpkin pie spice

    ½ teaspoon salt

    1 cup light brown sugar

    Whipped cream (optional)

Directions

1. Coat a 7-inch springform pan with non-stick cooking spray and then combine butter, chopped pecans, and cookie crumbs in a bowl.

2. Spread the crust evenly at the bottom and about an inch up the side of the pan and put in a freezer for 10 minutes.

3. To make the filling, mix together pumpkin pie spice, salt and sugar in a large bowl and then whisk in pumpkin, egg and evaporated milk.

4. Now pour the batter into the piecrust and cover the top of your spring-form using an aluminum foil.

5. Into the Instant Pot, add a cup of water and position the trivet at the bottom. Center the filled pan carefully on a foil sling and drop it into the cooking pot.

6. Fold the foil sling in order to prevent any interruption with the lid closing. Once set, lock the lid in place.

7. Cook for 35 minutes using "Manual" and "High Pressure" and then turn off the cooker after the beep sounds.

8. Release the pressure using a quick release, then remove the pie then cool for 7 minutes.

9. Now remove the springform pan to a wire rack in order to cool, and remove the aluminum foil.

10. 1Once the pie has cooled fully, cover with plastic wrap and keep refrigerated for approximately 4 hours. If desired, you can serve with some whipped cream.

Samoa Cheesecake

Serves 6

Ingredients

For Crust

    3 tablespoons butter melted

    1 cup chocolate graham cracker cookies, crushed

For Filling

    1 egg yolk, room temperature

    2 eggs, room temperature

    1 tablespoon all purpose flour

    2 teaspoons vanilla extract

    ¼ cup sour cream

    ½ cup heavy cream

    1 cup sugar

    12-ounces cream cheese

For Topping

    ½ cup semisweet chocolate, chopped

    4 tablespoons heavy cream

    12 chewy caramels, unwrapped

    2 cups sweetened coconut, shredded

Directions

1. Grease a 7 inch springform pan with non-stick cooking spray.

2. Combine butter and the cracker crumbs in a small bowl and then spread evenly in the bottom and the sides of the pan.

3. Keep refrigerated for around 10 minutes.

4. Mix together sugar and cream cheese in a mixing bowl at medium high speed until smooth; then blend in vanilla, heavy cream, flour, and sour cream.

5. Then mix in the eggs one by one, mix well and then transfer the batter into the pan over the crust. Use aluminum foil to cover the foil.

6. Pour a cup of water into the Instant Pot, and place a trivet at the bottom. Then center the pan onto a foil strip and drop it carefully into the inner pot.

7. Lock the lid and cook for 35 minutes using "Manual" and "High Pressure." Then turn off the Instant Pot and do a quick release.

8. Now remove the cheesecake to confirm whether the middle is set and ready; if not, cook for 5 minutes under "High Pressure".

9. Remove the pan from the wire rack to cool, then remove the foil and wait for the cheesecake to cool down.

10. Keep the cake in the fridge for 4 hours or alternatively overnight, then prepare the topping as the cheesecake chills.

11. Preheat an oven to 300 degree F, then spread coconut evenly on a baking sheet lined with parchment paper.

12. Toast it for 20 minutes, until the coconut turns golden in color, and then allow it to cool.

13. Once cool, put the cream and caramel into a bowl that is microwave safe and microwave for 1-2 minutes on high. Ensure you stir afterwards.

14. Once smooth, stir in your toasted chocolate and then spread the topping carefully over the top of the cheesecake.

15. Into a microwave safe bowl, melt chocolate as you stir regularly. Once melted put it into a Ziploc bag and snip off a little bit of the corner of the Ziploc bag.

16. Now drizzle over the top of the caramel topping.

Cheesecake with Shortbread Cookie Crust

Serves 8-10

Ingredients

For Crust

> 3 tablespoons butter melted
>
> 2/3 cup pecans, chopped
>
> 8 crushed shortbread toffee cookies

For Filling

> 3 eggs, room temperature
>
> 2 tablespoons all purpose flour
>
> 3 teaspoons vanilla extract
>
> 1/3 cup sour cream
>
> 2/3 cup heavy cream
>
> 2 cup sugar
>
> 2 (8-ounce) packages cream cheese

Directions

1. Grease a 7 inch springform pan with non-stick cooking spray.

2. Combine butter, chopped pecans, and crushed shortbread toffee cookies in a bowl. Spread evenly in the bottom and sides of the pan then refrigerate for around 10 minutes.

3. Mix sugar and cream cheese in a mixing bowl until smooth. Then blend in the flour, vanilla, heavy cream and the sour cream.

4. Now mix the eggs one at a time to fully incorporate then pour the batter onto the prepared crust.

5. Position the trivet in the bottom of the cooker, add in a cup of water and then drop the pan using a sling into the trivet. To make a sling, just fold an 18-20 inch aluminum foil 3 times lengthwise.

6. Lock the lid in place and cook for 30 minutes using "Manual" and "High Pressure". Once done, wait 15 minutes for a natural release then remove the can carefully.

7. Allow it to cool for 1-2 hours and then keep in the fridge for 2-3 hours or alternatively overnight.

8. Enjoy

Snacks

Crispy Potatoes

Serves 5

Ingredients

½ medium lemon

½ cup Italian parsley, minced

Black pepper, freshly grounded

Pinch of salt

3 tablespoons of ghee/butter

1.5 pound potatoes peeled and cut into cubes

Directions

1. Into an Instant Pot that is fitted with a steamer insert, add a cup of water and then dump in the potatoes.

2. Now seal the lid and select "Manual" and "High Pressure", and cook for 7 minutes.

3. Allow the pressure to release naturally for 10 minutes.

4. Select "Sauté" and cook the potatoes for 10 minutes, while mixing in ghee/butter. Stir often to prevent potatoes from burning.

5. Remove the potatoes from the Instant Pot and transfer onto a serving dish.

6. Now season with salt and pepper, squeeze the juice from half a lemon and toss in the parsley.

7. Enjoy

Refried Beans

Serves 4

Ingredients

3 cups of vegetable broth or water

Cilantro

1 cup salsa

1 teaspoon black pepper

1 teaspoon cumin

2 teaspoon chili powder

1 teaspoon paprika

1 teaspoon salt

1 jalapeno - seeded

4 cloves of garlic, peeled and minced

1 large onion, cut into fourths

2 cups of dried pinto beans, not soaked

Directions

1. Add all the ingredients into the Instant Pot, and stir well. Then close and seal the lid.

2. Select the "Bean/Chili" and allow it to cook for the default time of 30 minutes." After, allow 15 minutes of natural pressure release.

3. Open the lid and stir thoroughly. You can mash the beans using a potato masher.

4. Serve the fried beans warm with some nachos or freeze into portion-sized containers.

Mashed Acorn Squash

Serves: 4-6

Ingredients

½ cup water

¼ teaspoon baking soda

1 teaspoon salt

2 acorn squash, stem trimmed, cut in half, and seeded

For mix in

Salt and pepper

½ teaspoon grated nutmeg

3 tablespoons brown sugar

3 tablespoons butter

Directions

1. First sprinkle the cut side of the squashes with baking soda and salt.

2. Then place a cooking rack and steaming basket in an Instant Pot, and follow this with ½ cup of water. Now stack the squashes on top.

3. Lock the lid and then bring the Instant Pot to "High Pressure", using the "Manual" function. Cook the squash for 25 minutes.

4. Once done with cooking, quick release the pressure and remove the squashes from the cooker and allow it to cool for 5 minutes.

5. Now scrape the flesh from your squash into a medium bowl, and add in the nutmeg, brown sugar and butter.

6. With a potato masher, mash the squashes in order for the butter to melt and the squashes to become smooth.

7. Season with salt and pepper.

8. Enjoy

Vanilla Spice Poached Plums

Makes 3 cups

Ingredients

  1 ½ cups water

  3 tablespoons honey

  3 cardamom pods

  4 cloves

  3 cinnamon sticks

  1 star anise

  1 vanilla bean pod, split and seeded

  1 ½ pounds fresh plums (15 small ones)

Directions

1. Cut the plums into 2 halves, then remove the pit and put the contents into the bottom of the Instant Pot.

2. Split the vanilla bean into two halves lengthwise and scrape the seeds out of each half using a knife.

3. Add the 1½ cups water to the Instant Pot followed by the honey, spices, and the vanilla pod halves. Finally, seal the pot.

4. Select "Manual" and "High Pressure".

5. Now cook the contents for 18 minutes.

6. Allow the pressure to release naturally for 15 minutes then remove the lid.

7. You can now remove the plums. Heat the liquid using "Sauté" for 6-8 minutes until the remaining liquid is reduced in half.

8. Finally store the plums with the liquid in a glass jar (airtight) and then place in the fridge or serve the mixture over some yogurt and eat as is.

Yogurt

Serves 4

Ingredients

> 4 teaspoon live culture
>
> 4 cups milk
>
> 4 Glass jars that fit into the cooker

Directions

1. Pour in a cup of water into the Instant Pot.

2. Put the steamer rack in position, and then fill the four 1-cup jars with milk.

3. Position the jars (without the lids) into the cooker and seal the Instant Pot's lid in place.

4. Click on the "Steam" program, and "Adjust" the timer to 3 minutes. Allow the contents to cool down for 3 minutes, then do a quick release and open the cooker.

5. Lift the lid to let the milk to cool for another 3 minutes, and then remove the jars from the cooker.

6. Add in a teaspoon of the live culture yoghurt into each of the 4 glass jars.

7. Mix the ingredients well in order for the yoghurt culture to dissolve and then return the glass jars into the cooker.

8. Lock and now press the "Yoghurt" program and wait about 8 hours for the yoghurt processing to complete. A longer time is recommended as it makes the yoghurt tarter.

9. Once the time is up, the pressure cooker should display 'YOGT' which means that your yoghurt is ready.

10. You can solidify the yogurt in the fridge or serve as is.

11. Enjoy

Red Cabbage Salad

Serves 4

Ingredients

Salt and pepper

1 teaspoon brown sugar

2 teaspoons red wine vinegar

1 tablespoon canola oil

½ cup onion, chopped

2 cups red cabbage, shredded

Directions

1. In a steamer basket place the red cabbage and lower it into the Instant Pot.

2. Seal the lid of the cooker, then using "Manual" and "High Pressure", cook for 2 minutes followed by a quick release of the pressure.

3. Get the steamer out and cool by running cold water over the red cabbage and then transfer the cabbage into another bowl to add all the other ingredients.

4. Toss the contents and mix well, then serve. You can add more vinegar and oil to suit your preference.

German Potato Salad

Serves 4

Ingredients

½ teaspoon celery seed

Salt and pepper

1 medium onion, diced

4 medium-large potatoes cut in quarter inch slices

1 teaspoon mustard

3 tablespoons vinegar

5 teaspoons sugar

5 slices bacon

Directions

1. In the Instant Pot, fry the bacon until it is crisp, remove from the cooker, and drain on paper towels. Use the "Sauté" function here for 12 minutes.

2. Reserve 2 teaspoons of the drippings (Bacon Oil) and then wipe the pressure cooker.

3. Mix the reserved bacon drippings, mustard, vinegar and sugar in a small bowl and pour about 1¾ cups of water into the Instant Pot.

4. Dice the bacon, then in layers, arrange the onions and potatoes in the cooker and sprinkle the layers with the diced bacon, celery seed, pepper, salt and the vinegar-mustard mixture.

5. Now, seal the lid and select the "Manual" and "High Pressure" settings and cook for 15 minutes, followed by a natural release for 15 minutes.

6. Serve and enjoy

Conclusion

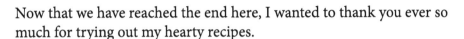

Now that we have reached the end here, I wanted to thank you ever so much for trying out my hearty recipes.

It is in my dear aspirations that this book was not only able to help you to learn how to use an Instant Pot but make tasty meals as well. The next thing you need to do is to start trying more of the recipes in this book and you will not be disappointed. Please leave a comment in the review section of this book on Amazon and let me know what you liked or didn't like.

Thank you, and to the inner chef in all of us, I wish you the best of luck.

Sincerely,

Madison Rose